This book belongs to

_____

Compassionate Ninja

By Mary Nhin

Pictures by
Jelena Stupar

Compassionate Ninja's heart raced as she thought about the first day of school.

While her mind went back and forth between scared and nervous, she spotted a heart shaped seashell.

Brave Ninja encouraged her to hold the seashell near her ear to see what it was saying. "If you listen closely, you can hear what it's trying to say much like how your real heart talks to you."

Compassionate Ninja brought the seashell close to her ear.
If she listened carefully, she *could* hear something...

The next day while getting dressed for school, she remembered what Brave Ninja told her. *Listen to your heart and try to hear what it tells you. If you do that, you'll do great.*

At recess, she noticed Hard-working Ninja sitting alone. She knew he didn't speak much English and he had even less friends than her.

With the seashell in her pocket, she rubbed it's rough edges thinking about how Hard-working Ninja might be feeling. She decided to invite him to play ball.

During class, Hangry Ninja forgot the markers she needed to complete the work Mrs. Smith assigned.

Compassionate Ninja rubbed her heart-shaped seashell and listened to her heart.

At soccer practice, Compassionate Ninja missed a goal.

Forgetting about her seashell, she muttered to herself,

Brave Ninja could tell she was upset and reminded her that listening to her heart included being kind to herself. "We should always be a good friend to ourselves, too."

Her friend was right. She had learned how to be kind to others but not so much to herself.

She made a promise to herself that from now on she would show herself some compassion, too.

The next day the teacher taught a new lesson and assigned the class some difficult work.

Compassionate Ninja had a hard time learning it.

Instead of muttering unkind things to herself, she remembered to speak kindly to herself, just as she would a friend.

She rubbed the hard edges of the heart-shaped seashell that was in her pocket and gently told herself,

You're still learning. It's okay to ask for help. As long as you try your best, you're doing great.

Compassionate Ninja's Promise

I promise to myself, on this very day
To try to be kind in every way
To every person, big or small,
I will help them one and all.
When I love myself, and others, too.
That is the best that I can do!

Compassion could be your secret weapon against unkindness.

Check out our fun, free printables at growgrit.co

@marynhin @GrowGrit
#NinjaLifeHacks

Mary Nhin Grow Grit

Grow Grit